Aidan is a writer and humour enthusiast with a deep passion for the culture and history of Northern Ireland. With roots in County Armagh and a keen ear for storytelling, he has spent years exploring the rich tradition of wit and humour that defines Northern Irish life. Through his work, Aidan brings to life the unique voices, stories, and laughter that have shaped the region, making readers feel as if they're sitting in a cozy pub, sharing a laugh with old friends.

This book is dedicated to my dad, Jimmy, whose love for music, laughter, and storytelling shaped my understanding of what it means to truly connect with people. As a talented singer in a band, he taught me the value of entertainment, the joy of making others smile, and the importance of sharing a moment through humour and song. His spirit lives on in every story and every laugh, and this book is a tribute to the warmth, humour, and love he brought into my life. Always missed, never forgotten.

Table of Contents

Introduction: The unique humour of Northern Ireland

Chapter 1: Antrim – Sharp tongues and legendary banter

Chapter 2: Armagh – Dry wit and clever storytelling

Chapter 3: Derry/Londonderry – Playful sarcasm and cultural humour

Chapter 4: Down – A blend of wit and warmth

Chapter 5: Fermanagh – Rural humour with a touch of quirkiness

Chapter 6: Tyrone – Earthy humour and a legacy of storytellers

Chapter 7: Bringing It all together – Humour in Northern Irish identity.

ACH, YOU UNS ARE BUCK EEJITS.

Introduction: The unique humour of Northern Ireland

Humour is an integral part of Northern Irish culture, woven into the very fabric of daily life. In a land steeped in history, marked by conflict, and known for its rugged landscapes, the people of Northern Ireland have developed a brand of humour that is as varied as it is distinctive. From the quick-witted banter of Belfast's streets to the dry, understated quips of the rural communities, Northern Irish humour acts as both a defence mechanism and a celebration of life.

The turbulent political history of Northern Ireland has undoubtedly shaped the humour of its people. In many ways, humour here is a coping mechanism, a way to diffuse tension and create unity in the face of adversity. But it's not all gallows humour or politically charged jokes. The humour of Northern Ireland is also grounded in the daily lives of its people, with a keen observational eye on the absurdities of human behaviour, a love of wordplay, and an innate sense of the ridiculous.

What sets Northern Irish humour apart from other forms of British or Irish humour is its ability to walk the fine line between light-hearted banter and sharp satire. It's both self-deprecating and fiercely proud, playful and biting. The diversity of Northern Irish humour is perhaps best understood by examining it county by county, as each region of this small but complex part of the world brings its own unique flavour to the table.

In this book, we'll take a journey through the six counties of Northern Ireland — Antrim, Armagh, Derry/Londonderry, Down, Fermanagh, and Tyrone — exploring the humour that defines each area. From the famous comedians who have emerged from these counties to the everyday exchanges between neighbours, this book will offer an in-depth look at the different types of humour that shape Northern Irish identity.

Northern Ireland's comedians have made an indelible mark not only on local culture but on the wider world of comedy. Figures like Frank Carson, Patrick Kielty, and Kevin McAleer have brought the wit and charm of

Northern Irish humour to international audiences. But beyond the professional comedians, it's the everyday interactions – the quick retorts, the playful teasing, the affectionate mockery – that truly encapsulate the heart of Northern Irish humour.

Each county has its own distinct way of making people laugh. In Antrim, the humour is sharp, fast-paced, and often biting. In Armagh, the jokes are more likely to come with a dry delivery, steeped in clever storytelling. Derry/Londonderry is known for its sarcastic wit, often used to poke fun at both sides of the political divide. In Down, you'll find a blend of wit and warmth, where the humour is gentle but never without bite. Fermanagh's humour is quirky and often shaped by the rural life, while in Tyrone, the humour is earthy, rich with tradition, and grounded in storytelling passed down through generations.

In the following chapters, we'll explore the historical and cultural contexts that have shaped the humour of each county. We'll dive into the slang, the famous comedic figures, and the stories and anecdotes that define what makes people from Antrim laugh differently from those in Armagh or Fermanagh. Through this journey, we'll uncover how humour has become not just a pastime but a way of life in Northern Ireland, a unifying force that transcends the political and religious divides that have so often defined the region.

So, grab a cup of tea (or perhaps a pint of Guinness), settle in, and get ready to embark on a comedic tour of Northern Ireland. You might just learn a new way to tell a joke, pick up a bit of slang, or discover why Northern Irish humour has a universal appeal that resonates far beyond the borders of this small but vibrant place.

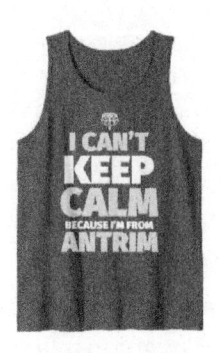

Chapter 1: Antrim – Sharp tongues and legendary banter

Antrim, home to Northern Ireland's bustling capital, Belfast, is where you'll find some of the sharpest tongues and fastest wits in the country. The humour here is known for being quick, cutting, and often laced with a good dose of sarcasm. It's a place where no conversation is safe from a biting one-liner, and banter is an art form in itself.

The legacy of humour in Antrim is deeply connected to its urban culture, particularly the city of Belfast. With its mix of working-class grit, political tension, and rapid urbanisation, Belfast has long been a breeding ground for a humour that is both tough and resilient. It's no wonder that some of Northern Ireland's most famous comedians, including the legendary Frank Carson, hailed from this area.

The legacy of Frank Carson: A Belfast icon

Frank Carson was perhaps the best-known comedian to come out of Antrim, and his humour perfectly encapsulates the spirit of the county. Born in Belfast in 1926, Carson rose to fame in the 1960s and 70s with his rapid-fire delivery, often punctuated by his catchphrase, "It's the way I tell 'em!" Carson's jokes were simple, often revolving around everyday life, but his timing and delivery were impeccable.

One of his best known jokes goes: A man walks into a pet shop and says: "Give me a wasp." The shopkeeper replies: "We don't sell wasps." He says: "There's one in the window."

Frank once slipped something into the pocket of a luggage handler at the airport and said: "Have a drink on me." The luggage handler later found out it was a tea bag.

Carson's humour was very much in line with the Belfast tradition – fast, funny, and often self-deprecating. He had a way of taking the everyday struggles of working-class life and turning them into something to laugh about. Whether it was making jokes about the weather, local politics, or the quirks of Belfast life, Carson had an ability to find humour in even the bleakest situations. His legacy lives on, not just in his jokes but in the way Belfastians continue to use humour as a way of coping with hardship and adversity.

The banter of Belfast: A way of life

Banter is a way of life in Belfast. It's fast, it's sharp, and it often toes the line between affection and insult. In many ways, banter is a form of social bonding in Antrim – if someone is teasing you, it's usually a sign of acceptance. But be warned: if you can't give as good as you get, you might struggle to keep up. The humour here is tough, but it's also playful, and there's an unspoken rule that nothing is ever meant to truly hurt.

A classic example of Belfast banter can be seen in the way people greet each other. A common greeting might be, "What's wrong with ye, ye look like death warmed up!" It's a backhanded compliment, meant to poke fun, but it's also a way of saying, "I care about you." This kind of humour, where the insult is wrapped in affection, is quintessentially Belfast.

Political humour: Defusing tension through laughter

Given Northern Ireland's complex political history, it's no surprise that political humour plays a significant role in Antrim's comedic landscape. During the Troubles, humour became a way to cope with the constant tension and fear that permeated daily life. Jokes about politics, religion, and the conflict were common, but they were often told in a way that defused the tension rather than exacerbating it.

One popular joke from the era goes: "A man walks into a bar in Belfast and says, 'I'm half Protestant and half Catholic.' The barman says, 'Aye, but which half do you want me to shoot first?'" It's dark humour, to be sure, but it's also a way of acknowledging the absurdity of the situation and finding a moment of levity in a deeply divided society.

The humour of Antrim is tough, sharp, and quick-witted, shaped by the urban life of Belfast and the challenges its people have faced over the years. In this chapter, we'll explore how this unique brand of humour has evolved, the role of famous comedians and how banter, slang, and political jokes continue to define the comedic landscape of the region.

Belfast slang: The backbone of local humour

A key component of Belfast humour, and Antrim humour more broadly, is the local slang. Language in Belfast is colourful, expressive, and often very specific to the area. Many of the jokes and banter revolve around the clever use of slang, with phrases that can be baffling to outsiders but are instantly understood by locals.

One of the most iconic Belfast phrases is "What's the craic?" ("Craic" means fun or news, and this phrase essentially means "How are you?" or "What's going on?"). It's a common greeting, but the word "craic" is versatile and can pop up in different contexts. For example, if someone says "The craic was mighty last night," it means they had a great time.

Another common phrase is "dead on," which means "fine" or "okay." If someone asks how you're doing and you reply, "I'm dead on," it means you're doing just fine. This kind of understated humour is very typical of Belfast.

There's a tendency to downplay things, even when they're going well, which adds to the charm of the people.

Some Belfast slang terms are more playful, like calling someone a "melter" (someone who is annoying) or "eejit" (fool or idiot). These terms are often used affectionately rather than as harsh insults. If someone calls you an "eejit," it's usually meant in good humour rather than as a genuine put-down.

The language in Belfast is full of these little quirks and turns of phrase that make everyday conversations feel like a comedic exchange. It's part of the charm of the city, where the line between a conversation and a comedy routine is often blurred.

Local legends and anecdotes: Humour in everyday life

Antrim, and especially Belfast, is a place where storytelling thrives. Whether it's the older generation reminiscing about the "good old days" or younger people sharing stories from a night out, humour is a constant companion. Everyday life in Belfast provides plenty of material for jokes and funny stories, and the locals have a natural talent for turning the mundane into the hilarious.

One such story that captures the essence of Belfast humour involves a famous bar in the city. Known for its lively atmosphere, the pub attracted a mix of regulars and tourists. One evening, a tourist asked the barman, "What's the secret to pulling a good pint of Guinness?" Without missing a beat, the barman replied, "A steady hand and a bit of prayer." The response got a big laugh, not only because of its wit but also because it perfectly captured the laid-back yet sharp humour that defines Belfast.

Another well-loved anecdote involves the local buses. Anyone who's been to Belfast knows that public transport can be a bit unpredictable. One day, a frustrated passenger asked the driver, "When's the next bus?" The driver, who had clearly had a long day, simply shrugged and said, "I've no idea, but I'll give you a shout when I see it coming." It's that blend of humour and practicality that makes Belfast such a unique place – even in moments of frustration, there's always room for a joke.

The humour of hardship: Finding laughter in difficult times

Belfast, like much of Northern Ireland, has had its share of hardships. From the Troubles to economic struggles, the people of Antrim have faced more than their fair share of challenges. But throughout it all, humour has remained a vital part of daily life. In fact, some of the best jokes come from the darkest moments, where laughter is used as a way to cope with adversity.

One of the most enduring aspects of Antrim humour is the ability to laugh at oneself. Self-deprecation is a hallmark of Northern Irish humour, and nowhere is this more evident than in Belfast. Whether it's making fun of the weather ("Sure, it's only raining slightly sideways today!") or poking fun at local politics, people in Antrim have a remarkable ability to find the humour in their own situation.

A common joke during the Troubles went something like this: "If you want to know who's a Protestant and who's a Catholic in Belfast, just ask them how they make their tea." It was a way of poking fun at the absurdity of the religious divide, showing that in the end, everyone was more alike than different, despite the tension.

Humour was also a way of showing resilience. During the darkest days of the Troubles, people would often use jokes to defuse tension or show that they weren't beaten by the violence. Even in the face of fear, laughter provided a sense of normalcy and a way to keep going. This use of humour as a coping mechanism is one of the defining features of Antrim's comedic landscape.

The rise of modern comedy in Antrim

While Belfast's streets have always been filled with banter, the rise of modern comedy has seen many talented comedians emerge from Antrim, bringing the county's unique humour to a wider audience. The comedy scene in Belfast is thriving, with stand-up shows, comedy clubs, and festivals becoming increasingly popular.

Patrick Kielty, one of Northern Ireland's most famous comedians, hails from Dundrum, County Down, but his work is closely tied to Belfast, where he started his career. Kielty's humour often revolves around Northern Irish life, particularly the politics and culture of the area. His ability to mix personal stories with political commentary, all delivered with a sharp wit, has made him a beloved figure in the comedy world.

Another modern comedian with strong ties to Antrim is Jake O'Kane. Known for his acerbic wit and no-holds-barred approach, O'Kane's humour is deeply rooted in the experiences of growing up in Belfast. His stand-up routines often explore the absurdities of Northern Irish life, from the weather to the political situation, and he's known for his ability to make even the most serious topics funny.

The growing popularity of comedy clubs in Belfast, such as The Empire Laughs Back, has provided a platform for up-and-coming comedians to showcase their talent. These venues have become an important part of the city's cultural fabric, drawing audiences who are eager to laugh at themselves and their shared experiences.

One particular comedian who is making waves in the NI comedy scene is "Belfast Giant" Ciaran Bartlett. One of Belfast's standout comedic voices, has quickly made a name for himself with his sharp, often biting humour and his remarkable ability to capture the essence of Northern Irish life. Known for his irreverent take on everything from daily struggles to the absurdities of modern living, Bartlett's humour is deeply rooted in the experience of growing up in Belfast. His comedy blends observational wit with a healthy dose of self-deprecation, often skewering the frustrations of living in a divided city with humour that resonates far beyond Belfast's borders.

Bartlett's style is a mix of cutting sarcasm and unfiltered honesty, making him a refreshing presence in the Northern Irish comedy scene. He frequently draws on the quirks of Belfast life in his routines, offering hilarious insights into local politics, social dynamics, and the peculiarities of the city's culture. Whether he's joking about the city's unpredictable weather, the infamous "Belfast approach" to customer service, or the everyday challenges of working-class life, Bartlett's humour is as relatable as it is uniquely Belfast.

What sets Ciaran Bartlett apart is his ability to handle complex and often difficult subjects with a balance of humour and sensitivity. In a city that has a history of tension, Bartlett isn't afraid to push boundaries, using humour as a tool to address social and political issues. However, he does this in a way that invites audiences to laugh together at shared experiences, making light of the heavy without losing the weight of the topic. His ability to navigate these fine lines has earned him a loyal following not only in Belfast but across Northern Ireland and beyond.

The future of Antrim's humour

As Belfast and County Antrim continue to evolve, so too does the humour that defines them. The city of Belfast, at the heart of Antrim, has undergone significant transformation in recent decades, moving from a history marked by political tensions to becoming a vibrant, modern city filled with creativity and cultural diversity. With these changes come new influences, perspectives, and stories that are reshaping the landscape of humour in Antrim. Yet, at the core of this evolution lies the unmistakable sharp-tongued banter and quick wit that has long been a hallmark of the county's comedic identity.

Antrim's humour has always been a mirror to the lives and struggles of its people. Historically, it has served as a tool for resilience, allowing communities to bond through laughter in the face of hardship. Whether during the political and social challenges of the Troubles or in navigating the everyday trials of working-class life, humour has been an essential part of Antrim's social fabric. This ability to find humour in adversity remains one of Antrim's greatest strengths. Even as the landscape changes and new comedic voices emerge, this sense of humour as a means of survival and connection endures.

The diversity in Belfast, and Antrim more broadly, is now richer than ever before. People from different backgrounds, cultures, and walks of life are contributing to the city's growing cosmopolitan identity. This brings with it new comedic perspectives and experiences, expanding the range of humour available to the people of Antrim. Immigrant communities, young artists, and a new generation of creative minds are blending their own unique experiences with Antrim's traditional humour, creating a comedy scene that is more varied, inclusive, and global in its outlook. Yet, no matter how broad the scope becomes, the local wit, with its sharp edge and affectionate teasing, will always remain central to Antrim's humour.

The rise of social media and digital platforms has also opened new avenues for humour to thrive in Antrim. Online, a new generation of Northern Irish comedians are finding their voice, sharing local jokes and observations with a global audience. Platforms like YouTube, TikTok, and Instagram have allowed Belfast-based comedians to quickly gain popularity far beyond the county's borders. Whether they are riffing on local slang, poking fun at Belfast's ever-changing skyline, or drawing humour from the particularities of Northern Irish politics, these comedians are bringing Antrim's humour to a wider, more diverse audience than ever before.

As the world becomes more interconnected, the comedy scene in Antrim is likely to continue evolving. However, what remains constant is the way humour is used as a tool for both connection and survival. In Antrim, humour is not just about making people laugh – it's about forming bonds, easing tensions, and finding common ground in a shared moment of levity. Whether it's a playful exchange with a stranger in the street or a comedian's one-liner defusing the weight of a political debate, humour in Antrim has a way of bringing people together in ways few other things can.

This is especially true in Belfast, where humour is often the first step toward breaking down barriers. In a city still working through the divisions of its past, humour has been a vital part of healing. Jokes allow people to navigate difficult conversations, helping them laugh together at the absurdities of life. This sharp, often self-deprecating humour acts as a balm, softening the edges of difficult experiences and allowing people to move forward.

Looking ahead, the future of Antrim's humour is bright. New generations of comedians are emerging, each bringing their own fresh voices, perspectives, and experiences to the stage. Some are continuing the proud tradition of sharp, sarcastic banter, while others are experimenting with new forms of comedy that blend elements of storytelling, political satire, and even absurdism. As these voices rise, they carry with them the legacy of the county's comedic past while pushing the boundaries of what humour can be in the modern world.

One thing is certain: the people of Antrim will continue to find joy and laughter, even in the most difficult of times. Humour remains a crucial part of life here – a way to say, "We're in this together," no matter what the circumstances. As new comedic stars emerge, they will undoubtedly carry forward Antrim's rich tradition of humour, ensuring that the county's reputation for wit, warmth, and laughter only grows stronger in the years to come.

In this sense, Antrim's humour is both timeless and adaptable. While the contexts may change, the heart of its comedy—its ability to laugh in the face of adversity and find humour in the everyday—will remain. The county's comedy scene will undoubtedly continue to flourish, producing new talent and sharing its unique blend of wit with the world. And in every laugh, there will be a reminder of the resilience, character, and cleverness that have long defined the people of Antrim.

As we conclude this chapter on Antrim's rich comedic tradition and look to the future, it's clear that humour will continue to play a pivotal role in the lives of its people. In the next chapter, we'll explore the wit and storytelling tradition of County Armagh, where dry humour and clever anecdotes take centre stage, reflecting a different but equally fascinating aspect of Northern Ireland's comedic identity.

> New York &
> Paris &
> Tokyo &
> Armagh

Chapter 2: Armagh – Dry wit and clever storytelling

If Antrim is known for its sharp banter and quick retorts, Armagh is the land of subtle humour and dry wit. The people of Armagh, often referred to as "the Orchard County," are masters of understatement and have a gift for turning even the most mundane stories into something worth listening to. This county, rich in history and culture, has its own unique approach to humour that revolves around clever storytelling, irony, and a deep sense of self-awareness.

In contrast to the fast-paced, often biting humour of Belfast, Armagh's comedy style is more reflective, filled with layers of meaning and understated punchlines. It's a type of humour that sneaks up on you, often with a dry delivery that leaves you chuckling long after the joke has been told. Whether it's a farmer spinning a tale about a "cursed" crop or a local pub regular regaling the crowd with stories of a hapless neighbour, the humour in

Armagh is rooted in observation and a deep understanding of the absurdities of everyday life.

The art of storytelling in Armagh

Storytelling is at the heart of Armagh's humour. In this rural county, where life can move at a slower pace, stories are passed down through generations, often becoming embellished over time. The best storytellers in Armagh have an uncanny ability to draw you in with their calm delivery and dry sense of humour, keeping you hooked until they hit you with the punchline, often with a straight face and a twinkle in their eye.

One famous anecdote from Armagh involves a local farmer known for his wit. When asked why he hadn't planted potatoes one particularly rainy year, he simply replied, "Sure, I didn't want to drown the poor things." The humour lies not in the answer itself, but in the delivery – dry, with a hint of exasperation, as though it were the most logical explanation in the world. It's this kind of understated humour that characterises much of Armagh's comedy.

The storytelling tradition in Armagh has also found its way into modern comedy, with comedians from the county drawing on their rural upbringing and the eccentric characters they've encountered over the years. Whether it's a tale about a local mechanic who "fixed" things by hitting them with a hammer or a story about a neighbour who claimed to have been abducted by aliens but only made it as far as the pub, Armagh's humour is full of these quirky, exaggerated tales that reflect the imagination and creativity of its people.

Armagh's comedic heritage: Mickey Bartlett

County Armagh may be known for its beautiful countryside, historical landmarks, and rich cultural traditions, but it has also produced some of Northern Ireland's most talented comedic minds. Among them is Mickey Bartlett, a standout in the Northern Irish comedy scene, whose sharp wit and irreverent humour have made him a favourite across the country and beyond. Bartlett's comedic style is firmly rooted in the unique blend of small-town charm and biting humour that defines much of Armagh's comedic heritage.

Born in Lurgan, a town with a strong working-class tradition, Mickey Bartlett grew up surrounded by the kind of people who could find humour in almost anything. His early life experiences—whether dealing with the ups and downs of life in a rural town, or the quirks of local characters—shaped the style of comedy he would later bring to the stage. Lurgan, like many small towns in Northern Ireland, offered Bartlett a wealth of material, from the oddities of local life to the uniquely Northern

Irish way of handling everyday frustrations with a joke or a cutting remark.

Bartlett first gained widespread attention on the comedy circuit in Northern Ireland for his sharp, observational humour and his ability to spin ordinary situations into laugh-out-loud stories. His humour often touches on relatable, everyday topics—like the awkwardness of growing up in a small town, the dynamics of family life, or the absurdities of politics and religion. What makes Bartlett's comedy resonate so strongly is his ability to mix dry wit with a healthy dose of self-deprecation, creating a sense of familiarity and connection with his audience.

In his comedy, Bartlett frequently references his upbringing in Lurgan, weaving stories about the people and experiences that shaped his view of the world. He has a gift for turning the challenges of small-town life into something hilariously relatable. For example, in one of his standout routines, Bartlett talks about the universal Northern Irish experience of going out for a few quiet drinks, only for the night to spiral into complete chaos. It's a situation familiar to many, but Bartlett's comedic timing and exaggerated storytelling elevate the routine into a masterpiece of humour.

He also doesn't shy away from poking fun at the stereotypes associated with growing up in a place like Lurgan. Whether it's the gossiping neighbours, the peculiar local characters, or the trials of dating in a small town where everyone knows everyone, Bartlett turns the idiosyncrasies of life in Armagh into comedic gold.

Another key aspect of Mickey Bartlett's humour is his willingness to dive into more sensitive topics—like politics, religion, and social issues—while maintaining his trademark irreverence. His comedy doesn't just aim for laughs; it often carries a pointed commentary on the absurdities of Northern Irish society. Whether discussing the complex political landscape or the quirks of living in a post-Troubles Northern Ireland, Bartlett has a knack for handling heavy subjects with a light touch, ensuring his humour never alienates but instead brings people together through shared laughter.

Bartlett's comedy has broad appeal, not only for those familiar with Northern Ireland's specific issues but for anyone who enjoys clever, relatable humour. He masterfully balances humour and insight, drawing out the ridiculousness of everyday situations while reflecting on the deeper social and cultural forces at play in Northern Irish life.

In many ways, Mickey Bartlett represents a bridge between the old tradition of Northern Irish storytelling and modern stand-up comedy. Like many of the comedians before him, Bartlett's routines are rooted in storytelling—he takes his audience on a journey, building up the narrative before delivering a punchline that feels both surprising and inevitable. This is a hallmark of Armagh humour: the ability to take a seemingly mundane story and turn it into something memorable, often with a dry, ironic twist.

While Bartlett is a rising star in the Northern Irish comedy scene, he is also a proud product of Armagh's long tradition of humour. The dry wit, observational storytelling, and quick banter that define Bartlett's style are all part of a broader comedic heritage that has been passed down through generations. His ability to capture the essence of life in Northern Ireland—its quirks, its contradictions, and its resilient sense of humour—makes him one of Armagh's most compelling comedic voices.

Another Lurgan reference arrived in the form of Sean Hegarty (also known as 'Rodney'), who, in 2017, won a competition to find Irelands funniest joke. The contest run by the Hardy Har Comedy Club in Bray had more than 2,000 votes cast.

And his joke...

'Do you think if one Domino's Pizza place were to close down, all the rest would have to follow?'

...came out on top of the pile among 450-plus other gags.

Classic Armagh!

Local humour: Everyday life in Armagh

The humour in Armagh often comes from the small, everyday moments of life in a rural community. Whether it's a farmer commenting on the weather or a shopkeeper sharing a joke with a customer, the humour here is often understated but sharp, with a keen sense of irony and a deep appreciation for the absurd.

Take, for example, the way people in Armagh talk about the weather. In a county where rain is a near-constant presence, the locals have developed a knack for making jokes about the unpredictability of the climate. A common phrase you might hear is, "If you don't like the weather in Armagh, just wait five minutes – it'll be something else entirely." This kind of dry, observational humour is typical of the region, where people have learned to laugh at the little inconveniences of life.

Another classic example of Armagh's everyday humour can be found in the local pubs, where patrons often engage in friendly banter with the barman or each other. One regular at a pub in Armagh was known for his constant complaints about the state of the world. One evening, after a particularly long rant about the price of groceries, the barman leaned over and said, "Sure, if complaining was an Olympic sport, you'd have a gold medal by now." The regular paused, considered this, and replied, "Aye, but they'd probably charge me for it!" It's this kind of playful, self-deprecating humour that defines the interactions between people in Armagh.

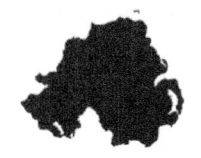

The slang of Armagh: Subtle and expressive

Armagh's humour is often expressed through its rich use of local slang, which, while not as brash as Belfast's, is full of subtlety and nuance. Phrases like "Aye, dead on" (used to express agreement, but often with a hint of sarcasm) or "That's grand" (which can mean anything from "That's fine" to "I couldn't care less") are staples of everyday conversation in Armagh.

One phrase that captures the essence of Armagh's humour is "That'll do rightly," which is used to indicate that something is sufficient or acceptable, but often with a wry smile that suggests it's not quite up to par. For example, if someone offers you a cup of tea and asks if it's strong enough, you might reply, "That'll do rightly," even if it's weak enough to be mistaken for dishwater. The humour lies in the delivery — it's not about what's said, but how it's said.

This kind of understated, almost passive-aggressive humour is common in Armagh, where people often use humour as a way to avoid confrontation or to make light of a situation without being overly direct. It's a type of humour that requires you to listen carefully, as the joke is often hidden beneath the surface.

Another term frequently used in Armagh is "oul doll," a phrase that can refer to either an old woman or, affectionately, to one's partner. The phrase has a playful, teasing quality to it, and it's often used in a humorous way. For example, a man might refer to his wife as "the oul doll" when recounting a story about her to his friends in the pub, knowing that it will get a laugh.

Humour and history: A legacy of resilience

Like much of Northern Ireland, Armagh has a complex history, marked by political and religious conflict. However, despite these challenges, the people of Armagh have maintained a strong sense of humour, using it to build resilience and maintain a sense of community.

During the Troubles, humour played an important role in helping people cope with the tension and uncertainty of daily life. Jokes about the absurdity of the political situation were common, and many of these jokes were delivered with the dry, understated wit that Armagh is known for.

One joke from the era goes: "A man walks into a pub in Armagh and asks the barman, 'Is this a Catholic pub or a Protestant pub?' The barman looks him up and down and says, 'Sure, we're just here for the drink.'" This kind of humour, which pokes fun at the divisions while also highlighting the commonalities, reflects the way people in Armagh used humour to rise above the conflict and find a sense of normalcy in difficult times.

The future of humour in Armagh

As Armagh continues to change and evolve, so too does its humour. While the rural traditions of storytelling and dry wit remain strong, there is a growing comedy scene in the county, with new voices emerging who are putting their own spin on the classic Armagh style.

Local comedy nights and storytelling events are becoming increasingly popular, providing a platform for up-and-coming comedians to showcase their talent. These events often combine traditional storytelling with modern stand-up comedy, creating a unique blend of old and new that reflects the changing face of Armagh's humour.

Whether it's through a clever story told in a local pub or a stand-up routine that blends dry wit with modern observations, the humour of Armagh continues to thrive. As new generations of storytellers and comedians emerge, they carry forward the legacy of clever, understated humour that has long been a defining feature of this county.

In the next chapter, we'll travel to County Derry/Londonderry, where playful sarcasm and a rich cultural history have shaped a unique form of humour that is as biting as it is charming.

Chapter 3: Derry/Londonderry – Playful sarcasm and cultural humour

If there's one thing that Derry/Londonderry is known for, aside from its striking walls and rich history, it's the razor-sharp wit and playful sarcasm that defines the humour of its people. Derry, often referred to simply as "the Walled City," has a distinctive comedic style that blends quick retorts, biting irony, and a willingness to poke fun at just about anything—especially themselves. The city's humour is as resilient as its walls, a testament to the spirit of a place that has seen more than its fair share of political and social upheaval.

Derry's humour is a powerful tool for social connection. It has long been a way for the city's residents to navigate the challenges of daily life, from the tensions of the Troubles to the more mundane frustrations of weather, politics, and family dynamics. But what sets Derry apart is the unapologetically bold and sarcastic flavour of its humour. The people here are quick to call out pretension, eager to highlight the absurdities of life, and always ready with a clever quip or a sharp comeback.

The roots of Derry's humour: A history of irony and resilience

Derry has a complex and often painful history, particularly during the Troubles, when the city became a focal point for conflict between nationalists and unionists. Despite—or perhaps because of—these difficulties, humour became a means of survival, a way for people to cope with the tension that seemed to hang over the city like a permanent cloud. The ability to laugh in the face of adversity, to find a moment of levity even in the darkest times, is one of the hallmarks of Derry's comedic tradition.

Sarcasm, in particular, has deep roots in Derry's humour. The city's residents are masters of the art of saying one thing while meaning the opposite, often in a way that's so subtle that outsiders might not catch on right away. This kind of humour requires a quick wit and a keen sense of timing, and the people of Derry have both in abundance.

One popular story in Derry involves a local man who, during the height of the Troubles, was stopped at a military checkpoint. When asked if he had any weapons or explosives in his car, he replied, "Sure, doesn't everyone?" The sarcasm was as much a defence mechanism as a way to inject a little humour into a tense situation. It's this kind of dry, cutting humour that Derry is famous for—sharp, sometimes risky, but always delivered with a twinkle in the eye.

Famous comedians from Derry: A tradition of quick wit

Derry has produced its fair share of comedians who have taken the city's distinctive humour to a wider audience. Perhaps the most famous is Derry Girls creator Lisa McGee, whose hit TV show has brought the humour of Derry to an international audience. The show, set during the 1990s in the midst of the Troubles, perfectly captures the combination of absurdity, sarcasm, and heart that defines Derry's comedy.

"Derry Girls" showcases the ability of the city's residents to find humour in difficult situations, whether it's dealing with a bomb scare on the way to school or navigating the often-awkward dynamics of family life. The characters' sharp tongues and quick-witted banter are classic examples of Derry's comedic style—fast, funny, and not afraid to say the unsayable.

But McGee isn't the only comedic talent to emerge from Derry. Diona Doherty is a rising comedic star from

Derry/Londonderry, known for her sharp wit, relatable humour, and versatility as both a stand-up comedian and an actress. With a distinct Northern Irish charm, Doherty's comedy often tackles the realities of modern life, from the challenges of growing up in Derry to the everyday absurdities of relationships and adulthood. Her humour is refreshingly honest and often self-deprecating, resonating with audiences across Ireland and beyond. Beyond stand-up, she's also a familiar face from her roles on television, including the popular BBC show Soft Border Patrol and her appearances on The Blame Game, where her quick wit and observational humour continue to win over new fans.

Everyday humour: Derry's street-level banter

While famous comedians have helped put Derry's humour on the map, the real heart of the city's comedy lies in its everyday banter. Whether it's in the pubs, on the streets, or in family homes, the people of Derry are always ready with a joke or a sarcastic comment, often delivered with a deadpan expression that makes it all the more hilarious.

In Derry, no topic is off-limits when it comes to humour, and people are just as likely to make fun of themselves as they are of anyone else. Self-deprecating humour is a key feature of the city's comedic style, with locals frequently making light of their own flaws, shortcomings, or the peculiarities of life in the city. If the weather's terrible—which it often is—you'll hear someone say, "Ah, sure, it's just a wee bit of rain!" even as they're soaked to the bone. If the traffic's bad, someone will quip, "At least we've got time for a wee chat." This kind of humour turns inconvenience into something to laugh about, rather than something to get upset over.

Another hallmark of Derry's humour is its willingness to push boundaries. The people here aren't afraid to be a little bit cheeky or to make a joke that might make others squirm. It's all done in good fun, though, and there's a strong sense of camaraderie behind the banter. In Derry, if someone's poking fun at you, it's usually a sign that they like you.

Local slang: A language of Its own

The people of Derry have a unique way of speaking, with a dialect and slang that's full of character and humour. Much like Belfast, Derry's local language is often used to inject humour into everyday conversations, and some of the most iconic phrases have become synonymous with the city's comedic identity.

One of the most famous Derry expressions is "What about ye?" which is a casual way of saying, "How are you?" It's often followed up with, "Aye, grand," even if the person in question isn't actually feeling all that grand. This kind of understated humour is typical of the region—people in Derry tend to downplay things, whether it's the weather, their own feelings, or the state of the world.

Another classic Derry phrase is "wee," which can be used to describe just about anything, regardless of its actual size. You might hear someone talk about their "wee house" (even if it's a fairly large house), their "wee car" (even if it's a massive SUV), or their "wee pint" (because any pint in Derry is better with a bit of humour thrown in). The use of "wee" adds a touch of lightness to any conversation, making even serious topics feel a little less heavy.

And then there's "catch yourself on," a phrase that's used to tell someone to stop being silly or to get a grip on reality. It's often said with a smile, even when it's meant seriously, and it's a perfect example of the way people in Derry mix humour with practical advice. If someone's getting too worked up about something minor, you might hear, "Catch yourself on!"—a reminder that life's too short to take things too seriously.

Anecdotes from Derry: Laughing through life's challenges

Derry's history of conflict has given rise to a wealth of humorous anecdotes, many of which reflect the city's ability to find laughter in even the most difficult circumstances. One well-known story from the Troubles involves a local man who was caught in the middle of a riot. As the police fired rubber bullets and protesters threw rocks, he calmly walked through the chaos with a newspaper over his head, as if it were an umbrella. When asked later why he did it, he simply said, "I didn't want to get caught in the rain." It's this kind of absurd, deadpan humour that defines the way Derry residents deal with tough situations.

Another popular story involves a local priest who, during the height of the Troubles, was giving a sermon about peace and forgiveness. As he was speaking, a bomb went off nearby, causing the windows of the church to rattle. Without missing a beat, the priest paused and said, "Well, that's one way to get their attention." The congregation burst into laughter, grateful for a moment of levity in the midst of the tension.

These kinds of stories are a testament to the resilience of Derry's people, who have always found ways to laugh even when times were tough. Humour has been a crucial part of the city's coping mechanism, helping to diffuse tension and bring people together, even in the darkest of times.

The future of Derry's humour: A new generation of comedians

As Derry continues to grow and evolve, so too does its humour. The city is home to a vibrant comedy scene, with new comedians emerging who are putting their own spin on Derry's traditional sharp wit and sarcasm. Comedy nights, open mic events, and festivals are increasingly popular, providing a platform for up-and-coming comedians to showcase their talent and bring fresh perspectives to the stage.

As new voices continue to emerge from the city, Derry's comedic tradition remains as strong as ever. Whether through stand-up comedy, television, or everyday banter on the streets, the people of Derry will always find a way to make each other laugh. It's a city where humour isn't just entertainment—it's a way of life, a way to connect with others, and a way to navigate the ups and downs of everyday existence.

In the next chapter, we will move to County Down, where a quieter, more reflective humour reigns—full of gentle teasing, irony, and a love for storytelling that mirrors the scenic beauty of the region.

I DRANK SOME WINE
AND I FELL DOWN

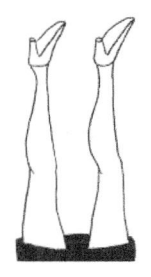

Chapter 4: County Down – A blend of wit and warmth

County Down, known for its lush landscapes and serene shores, offers a more tranquil setting than its neighbours, and this quiet beauty is reflected in the local sense of humour. In contrast to the biting sarcasm of Derry/Londonderry or the sharp banter of Antrim, Down is a place where humour is more subtle and reflective. The jokes here are rarely harsh or confrontational, often delivered with a gentle tease or an ironic twist, and there's an easy-going, laid-back feel to the way people interact.

While the pace of life in Down might be slower, the humour is by no means dull. It thrives on understatement, irony, and clever storytelling, with locals often laughing at themselves and the absurdities of daily life. Much like the landscape that inspires it, the humour in Down is calm but full of depth—always with a sense of warmth and a wink.

The tradition of gentle teasing in County Down

In Down, teasing is a key part of the local sense of humour, but it's done in such a way that it rarely feels mean-spirited. The people here have a knack for poking fun at each other in a way that feels affectionate, rather than cutting. Whether it's a playful dig at someone's tendency to exaggerate or a gentle ribbing about a friend's gardening skills (or lack thereof), the humour is light-hearted and rarely crosses into cruelty.

One popular form of humour in Down involves teasing someone for their local pride. Each village and town in Down seems to have its own fierce identity, and the locals are always ready to joke about the quirks of neighbouring places. For instance, people from Newcastle might poke fun at the residents of Bangor for their "big city ways," while those in Banbridge might tease those from Holywood for being a bit too posh. These jokes, though, are always delivered with a smile and an underlying sense of camaraderie—everyone knows it's all in good fun.

An anecdote from Down illustrates this well. In a small village outside Downpatrick, a local man was known for his tall tales, always exaggerating about the size of his fish catches or the quality of his homegrown vegetables. His friends, well aware of his tendency to stretch the truth, would often tease him with a straight face. One day, after he bragged about catching a fish "the size of a small boat," one of his friends replied, "Aye, and did it tow the boat back to shore for you as well?" The group erupted in laughter, and even the storyteller himself joined in. It's this kind of teasing, where everyone is in on the joke, that characterises humour in Down.

Storytelling: A quiet art in County Down

In County Down, humour often takes the form of quiet, reflective storytelling. The people here have a way of spinning tales that start off seeming perfectly ordinary, only to take a humorous turn halfway through, leaving the listener laughing at the unexpected punchline. The stories themselves aren't always laugh-out-loud funny, but they're filled with wit, irony, and a deep appreciation for life's small absurdities.

The local pubs in Down are the perfect places to hear this kind of storytelling in action. On a quiet evening, you might find an older man leaning on the bar, recounting a tale about a sheep that managed to escape its pen and wander into a local wedding, or a woman telling the story of how she once mistook a flock of swans for her husband's new coat flapping on the washing line. The humour in these stories isn't in the events themselves, but in the way they're told—with a slow build-up, careful attention to detail, and a final twist that leaves everyone smiling.

One legendary storyteller from County Down was a farmer named Hugh McArdle, who was known for his long, meandering tales that would eventually end in a punchline you never saw coming. One of his most famous stories involved a goose that he claimed could predict the weather. According to McArdle, the goose would honk every time rain was on the way, and it never once got it wrong. The punchline came when McArdle revealed, after much build-up, that the goose only ever honked when it saw the farmer coming down the lane with an umbrella. McArdle's deadpan delivery and the sheer ridiculousness of the story made it a hit, and people would come from miles around just to hear him tell it again.

Comedians from County Down: Masters of subtle comedy

While County Down may not be known for producing as many high-profile comedians as Belfast or Derry, its contribution to the world of humour is not to be overlooked. The comedians from this region often share the subtle, understated style of humour that is characteristic of Down, preferring clever wordplay and gentle irony over overt slapstick or biting satire.

One of the most beloved comedians from County Down is Patrick Kielty, who hails from Dundrum. Kielty's comedy, much like the humour of his home county, is marked by its charm, wit, and cleverness. He has a gift for making people laugh without being offensive or aggressive, and his routines often focus on the quirks of Northern Irish life, politics, and identity. Though he's known for his quick wit and sharp commentary, Kielty's humour always has a warmth to it—a reflection of the friendly teasing that's so central to Down's comedic tradition.

Kielty's style of comedy often involves subtle observations about the differences between Northern Ireland and the rest of the world, and he has a talent for finding humour in situations that others might find mundane. One of his most famous jokes involves him explaining the Northern Irish obsession with tea: "You know you're in Northern Ireland when you hear someone ask, 'Would you like a cup of tea?' and it's not really a question. It's more of an order, because there's no such thing as saying no to tea here." This kind of observational humour, grounded in everyday life, is a hallmark of Down's comedic style.

Local slang and humour in Down: The language of wit

Like the rest of Northern Ireland, County Down has its own unique slang, and this language plays a big role in the local sense of humour. Words and phrases that might seem confusing to outsiders are used in clever, often ironic ways, adding an extra layer of humour to everyday interactions.

One classic phrase you'll hear in Down is "away on," which is used to dismiss something as nonsense or exaggeration. For example, if someone were to say, "I caught a fish this big," they might be met with a sceptical "away on" from their friends, indicating that they're not buying the story. It's a gentle way of calling someone out, delivered with a smile and a raised eyebrow.

Another common expression in Down is "dead on," which can mean anything from "okay" to "good enough." It's often used in situations where someone is trying to downplay their excitement or satisfaction, in a typically understated Northern Irish way. For instance, if someone were to receive a compliment on their cooking, they might respond with, "Aye, dead on," even if they're secretly very pleased. The humour in this kind of understatement is subtle but sharp, and it reflects the laid-back, down-to-earth nature of the people here.

In County Down, humour also often revolves around irony. For example, locals might describe a day of torrential rain as "a wee bit of drizzle," or refer to a massive, unexpected snowfall as "a bit nippy out." This tendency to understate everything is a key part of the county's humour, and it's one of the reasons why people here are so adept at finding the funny side of even the most frustrating situations.

Anecdotes from Down: Finding humour in everyday life

The gentle humour of County Down shines through in the stories that locals tell about their day-to-day lives. These anecdotes often focus on the small, seemingly insignificant moments that, when told with the right mix of irony and wit, become hilarious.

One popular story from Down involves a local man who was known for his habit of accidentally locking himself out of his house. After the third or fourth time it happened, his neighbour started jokingly calling him "Houdini," teasing him about his apparent ability to escape from anywhere—except his own home. The nickname stuck, and soon everyone in the village was calling him Houdini, even though his only "magic trick" was his repeated forgetfulness.

Another well-loved anecdote from County Down is about a local postman who, after years of delivering letters to the same small community, became so familiar with the residents that he didn't even need the addresses anymore. He could simply glance at the handwriting and know exactly who the letter was meant for. When asked how he managed to keep track of so many people's letters, he would shrug and say, "Ah, sure, it's only a few of us. Besides, half of them write like they're using their feet!" This kind of dry, self-deprecating humour is typical of Down, where people often find ways to laugh at the little quirks and challenges of everyday life.

Humour and history: The peaceful reflection of Down

Unlike some of the other counties in Northern Ireland, Down has largely avoided the more intense conflict that has affected places like Derry or Belfast. As a result, its humour is often more reflective and less combative, focusing on the absurdities of daily life rather than political tensions or social divisions.

However, this doesn't mean that Down's humour is without depth. The people here are keenly aware of the world around them, and their humour often reflects a deep understanding of the complexities of life. The humour of Down is full of quiet wisdom, using irony and understatement to make subtle points about the nature of human experience.

This reflective quality is perhaps best seen in the way people from Down deal with the weather, which is a frequent topic of conversation—and humour—in the county. With the region's notoriously unpredictable climate, locals have developed a knack for making light of the constant rain and occasional storms. A common joke is that Down only has two seasons: winter and "a bit less winter." This kind of humour, which turns a frustrating reality into something to laugh about, is a perfect example of the way people in Down use humour to cope with life's challenges.

The future of humour in County Down

As County Down continues to grow and change, its humour evolves with it. New comedians and storytellers are emerging from the county, bringing fresh perspectives to the local comedy scene while still maintaining the gentle wit and irony that has long defined humour in this part of Northern Ireland.

The county's laid-back attitude and love of storytelling ensure that humour will always play a central role in the lives of its residents. Whether it's in a local pub, at a family gathering, or in the everyday banter between friends, the people of Down will continue to find ways to laugh at themselves and the world around them.

Next, we turn to County Fermanagh, where the humour takes on a reflective, almost philosophical quality, shaped by the county's lakes, rivers, and quiet rural beauty. Here, the humour is often slow, deliberate, and full of thoughtful observations about life and nature.

Chapter 5: County Fermanagh – Rural humour with a touch of quirkiness

Nestled in the southwest of Northern Ireland, County Fermanagh is a land of lakes, rivers, and serene beauty. The landscape here is dotted with quiet villages, ancient monastic sites, and crumbling castles, giving it a timeless, almost meditative feel. The humour of Fermanagh, like its landscape, is slow, thoughtful, and reflective, often shaped by the stillness of the lakes and the closeness of nature. It's a humour that pauses to consider life's ironies before delivering its punchline, full of careful observation and dry wit.

Unlike the boisterous humour of County Armagh or the rapid-fire banter of Belfast, Fermanagh's humour comes with a quiet smile, a knowing glance, and a subtlety that can be easily missed if you're not paying attention. The people of Fermanagh, known for their introspective nature, often use humour to explore the deeper truths of life, weaving their jokes with wisdom and a philosophical outlook.

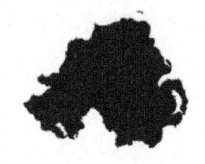

The quiet humour of the lakes

Fermanagh's famous lakes, particularly Lough Erne, play a central role in the county's identity, and naturally, much of the local humour is tied to the water. Boating, fishing, and rural life on the shores of the lakes are rich sources of humour, with locals often using the unpredictable nature of the water as a metaphor for the unpredictability of life itself.

One well-known local story involves a fisherman who spent a whole day on Lough Erne without catching a single fish. As he packed up his gear, a passerby called out, "How's the fishing?" The fisherman, without missing a beat, replied, "Oh, it's great—I've just been giving the fish a bit of exercise today!" The dry humour, with its understated delivery, perfectly captures the Fermanagh approach to life: roll with the punches, and find a reason to smile, even when things don't go as planned.

This kind of humour, which often involves a wry acceptance of life's unpredictability, is typical of the county. Locals enjoy poking fun at themselves and their rural lifestyle, using humour as a way to cope with the quiet challenges of living in such a remote and peaceful part of the world. Whether it's a joke about the weather turning on a dime or a quip about the slow pace of life, Fermanagh's humour always has a philosophical edge.

Comedians from Fermanagh: Storytellers with a reflective twist

Though Fermanagh is known for its serene landscape, it has also produced its share of comedians who bring that reflective quality to their performances. These comedians often rely on storytelling, painting vivid pictures of life in Fermanagh with humour that emerges from the small, everyday moments.

One of the most notable names associated with Fermanagh's humour is Frank Carson, who, while more famously linked with Belfast, had roots in County Fermanagh through his family. Carson was known for his rapid-fire delivery, but his humour always retained a certain depth, rooted in his sharp observations of people and life

Another comedian who embodies the thoughtful humour of Fermanagh is Colin Murphy, who has a deep understanding of rural life and uses it to craft jokes that blend wit with wisdom. While Murphy is not exclusively tied to Fermanagh, his style—a mix of observation, introspection, and a good dose of self-deprecation—resonates strongly with the county's unique brand of humour. His material often touches on the slow pace of rural life, the peculiarities of small-town living, and the sometimes absurd relationship between people and nature.

Fermanagh's dry wit: Humour in everyday conversations

Much of the humour in County Fermanagh comes not from big performances, but from the small, seemingly insignificant conversations that happen in daily life. In the pubs, on the farms, and by the lakes, people share stories, jokes, and observations that reveal a deep understanding of human nature and the world around them.

One common feature of Fermanagh's humour is its reliance on understatement. In a place where life moves slowly and people have plenty of time to reflect, the humour is often delivered with a straight face, allowing the punchline to land softly but powerfully. This kind of dry humour can be disarming, as it often catches you off guard with its subtlety.

For instance, it's not unusual to hear a Fermanagh farmer remark on the weather with a phrase like, "It's a grand soft day"—a typical euphemism for a day that's wet and miserable. The comment, delivered with a smile, is a way of acknowledging the reality of life in Fermanagh while also making light of it. There's an unspoken understanding that complaining won't change anything, so you might as well find a reason to laugh.

Another popular saying in Fermanagh is, "Sure, it could be worse," often used in response to even the most difficult situations. Whether someone's tractor has broken down in the middle of a field or they've spent hours out on the lake without catching a single fish, this phrase captures the county's resilience and ability to find humour in adversity. It's a way of acknowledging that life isn't always easy, but that there's always something to be grateful for—or at least, something to laugh about.

Slang and local expressions: The language of Fermanagh humour

As with every county in Northern Ireland, Fermanagh has its own unique set of slang words and expressions that reflect the local culture and way of life. These words are often used to add a layer of humour to everyday conversations, and they play a key role in the county's distinctive brand of wit.

One common phrase in Fermanagh is "auld hand," which refers to someone who is experienced or knowledgeable, particularly in practical matters like farming or fishing. This term is often used in a playful, teasing way, especially when someone is acting like they know more than they actually do. For example, if a young fisherman tries to give advice to an older, more experienced fisherman, the older man might respond with, "Ah, sure, he's an auld hand at it," with a twinkle in his eye.

Another frequently heard expression is "giving it welly," which means putting in a lot of effort or energy, often in a physical task. In a place like Fermanagh, where people are used to hard work on the land or on the water, this phrase is often used humorously to describe someone who is going all out—whether they're digging a garden or rowing a boat. For example, a farmer might joke, "He was giving it welly, but the tractor still wouldn't start!"

Anecdotes from Fermanagh: Finding humour in quiet moments

Some of the best humour in Fermanagh comes from the quiet, often mundane moments of life. These anecdotes, passed down through generations, capture the essence of the county's humour: slow, thoughtful, and full of quiet wit.

One popular story involves a man who was known for his love of fishing, despite being notoriously bad at it. Every weekend, rain or shine, he'd be out on Lough Erne with his fishing rod, determined to catch something. His friends would often tease him about his lack of success, but he'd always respond with a smile and say, "It's not about the fish, it's about the thinking time." His attitude, a mix of resignation and contentment, perfectly captures the reflective quality of Fermanagh humour.

Another well-loved anecdote tells of a local postman who, while delivering mail to a particularly remote farm, was known to stop for a chat with the farmer every day. One day, after a long conversation, the postman finally said, "Well, I'd better be off—I've still got letters to deliver." The farmer, without missing a beat, replied, "Aye, but sure, they'll still be there tomorrow." The exchange, with its slow pace and dry humour, is a perfect example of the way people in Fermanagh find humour in the simple, everyday moments of life.

Humour and history in Fermanagh: Coping with change

Fermanagh, like the rest of Northern Ireland, has faced its share of challenges over the years. From economic difficulties to political upheaval, the people of Fermanagh have had to adapt to changing times while holding on to their traditions and way of life. Throughout it all, humour has been a constant source of resilience, helping people to navigate the ups and downs of life with a smile.

In many ways, the humour of Fermanagh reflects the county's history of quiet endurance. The people here are used to working hard, whether on the farms or on the water, and their humour often revolves around the small victories and defeats of everyday life. Whether it's a joke about the weather, a story about fishing, or a wry comment on the slow pace of rural life, the humour of Fermanagh is a way of making sense of the world and finding joy in even the most ordinary moments.

The reflective, philosophical nature of Fermanagh humour also speaks to the county's deep connection to its landscape. Surrounded by lakes, rivers, and rolling hills, the people of Fermanagh have developed a unique perspective on life, one that values quiet reflection and thoughtful observation. Their humour, like the landscape itself, is slow and steady, but full of depth and meaning.

In the next chapter, we explore County Tyrone, where the humour is robust and spirited, filled with boisterous energy and a deep sense of community. Tyrone's humour reflects the county's hardworking, no-nonsense attitude and is often delivered with a sharp tongue and a twinkle in the eye.

Chapter 6: County Tyrone – Earthy humour and a legacy of storytellers

County Tyrone, the largest of Northern Ireland's six counties, is a place known for its proud history, strong work ethic, and no-nonsense approach to life. Tyrone's humour, much like its people, is full of energy and spirit, often delivered with a sharp tongue, quick wit, and an unmistakable edge. While the humour in Tyrone can be biting, it's rarely mean-spirited—rather, it's an expression of the community's toughness, resilience, and ability to laugh in the face of adversity.

The humour in Tyrone is often fast-paced and direct, with a focus on banter, teasing, and playful insults. It's a style of humour that reflects the county's industrious character, and it's not uncommon for locals to engage in verbal sparring matches, each trying to outwit the other with clever remarks and quick comebacks.

This chapter delves into the unique brand of humour found in County Tyrone, exploring the historical roots of the county's wit, its comedians and storytellers, and the everyday humour that fills the pubs, markets, and workplaces of this vibrant region.

The banter of Tyrone: Verbal sparring at its best

In Tyrone, banter is a way of life. The people here are known for their quick tongues and even quicker wit, and nowhere is this more evident than in the playful verbal sparring that takes place between friends, family members, and even strangers. This kind of banter is a form of social bonding, where the goal is not to hurt but to entertain and challenge one another with clever quips and sarcastic remarks.

One popular saying in Tyrone is, "If you can't take a joke, you shouldn't have been born here." It's a reflection of the county's love of teasing and the expectation that everyone should be able to laugh at themselves. In Tyrone, no one is off-limits when it comes to humour—whether you're the local farmer, the shopkeeper, or even the parish priest, you can expect to be the subject of good-natured ribbing at some point.

A typical exchange in a Tyrone pub might go something like this:

"You're looking well, Joe—did you get lost on your way to the barbers?"

Joe, not missing a beat, replies, "No, I just figured it's cheaper to let the wind do the cutting for me."

This kind of back-and-forth, where each person tries to outdo the other with a clever comeback, is a hallmark of Tyrone humour. It's quick, it's sharp, and it keeps everyone on their toes. The key to surviving in Tyrone is being able to laugh at yourself as much as you laugh at others—if you can take the heat, you'll be welcomed into the fold with open arms.

Practical jokes and physical comedy: A tradition of laughter

While Tyrone is known for its verbal wit, practical jokes and physical comedy also play a big role in the county's humour. Growing up in Tyrone, children often learn the art of the prank from a young age, and it's not uncommon for local farmers or tradesmen to engage in elaborate practical jokes on one another. These pranks are usually good-natured, designed to provoke laughter and bring the community closer together.

One classic prank in Tyrone involves the "cow pat joke." In rural areas, where farming is a way of life, locals often play tricks on each other using the tools and resources of the trade. A well-known trick is to convince an unsuspecting victim that there's a "golden coin" hidden in a cow pat, only for them to dig through it and find nothing but muck. The laughter comes not from humiliating the victim, but from the shared absurdity of the situation—everyone knows the trick is coming, and the joke is in the willingness of the person to fall for it.

Another popular prank involves sending a newcomer to the local farm supply store to ask for a "long stand" or a "left-handed shovel," both of which, of course, don't exist. The victim is sent from store to store, each time being told, "Just wait here, we'll get it for you," until they realise they've been had. These kinds of pranks, like much of the humour in Tyrone, rely on a mix of cleverness and good-natured fun, with the goal being to bring people together in laughter.

Comedians from Tyrone: Bold performers with a sharp edge

Tyrone has produced some of Northern Ireland's most beloved comedians, known for their bold performances and sharp, cutting humour. These comedians often draw on the county's strong tradition of banter and practical jokes, delivering their material with a mix of confidence, energy, and irreverence.

In the modern era, comedian Kevin McAleer, who hails from Tyrone, has taken the county's tradition of storytelling and brought it to a wider audience. Known for his deadpan delivery and surreal sense of humour, McAleer's style is quintessentially Tyrone. His performances often involve long, meandering stories delivered in a slow, deliberate manner, with punchlines that feel almost incidental. His humour is steeped in irony, with an understated charm that has earned him a loyal following both in Northern Ireland and beyond.

McAleer's routines often draw on his experiences growing up in rural Northern Ireland, with tales of eccentric relatives, bizarre local customs, and the peculiarities of life in a small village. His ability to take these seemingly mundane topics and turn them into comedy gold is a testament to the storytelling tradition that runs deep in Tyrone's culture.

One of his most famous routines involves a story about his uncle, who believed that television was powered by "tiny men" inside the set. The uncle's increasingly elaborate explanations about how these men operated the TV became more and more absurd, yet McAleer's delivery remained completely deadpan, making the story all the more hilarious. This kind of humour – surreal, understated, and steeped in the ridiculousness of everyday life – is at the core of Tyrone's comedic identity.

Another notable comedian from Donaghmore, Co. Tyrone is Conor Grimes, who, along with his comedic partner Alan McKee, has become well-known for their hilarious takes on Northern Irish politics and culture. Grimes' humour often centres around the contradictions and complexities of life in Northern Ireland, using satire to comment on everything from the peace process to the quirks of rural life. His performances are sharp, witty, and always full of energy, reflecting the boisterous spirit of his home county.

Language and slang in Tyrone: The power of words

As with every county in Northern Ireland, the people of Tyrone have their own unique way of speaking, full of slang words and phrases that give their humour a distinctive flavour. The language here is fast, direct, and often laced with sarcasm, making it the perfect vehicle for the county's sharp-tongued wit.

One commonly used phrase in Tyrone is "wind your neck in," which is a way of telling someone to calm down or stop being so full of themselves. This phrase is often delivered with a smile, making it clear that the speaker isn't being harsh—just giving their friend a bit of a reality check. Another popular expression is "as thick as champ," a humorous way of calling someone a bit slow or dense, with "champ" referring to the traditional Irish dish of mashed potatoes and spring onions.

Another term that frequently pops up in Tyrone is "hallion," which refers to a mischievous or unruly person, often used in a teasing manner. For example, a parent might affectionately scold their child by saying, "You're some hallion, aren't you?" It's a way of acknowledging the child's mischief without being overly critical, reflecting the playful nature of Tyrone's humour.

The people of Tyrone also have a talent for using everyday words in humorous ways. A simple comment about the weather can become a comedic moment, with locals using phrases like "it's coming down in buckets" to describe heavy rain, or "it's a day for the ducks" when the weather is particularly miserable. These expressions, delivered with a straight face, add to the county's unique brand of humour, where even the most mundane topics can be turned into a source of laughter.

Anecdotes from Tyrone: Big laughs in small moments

Some of the best humour in Tyrone comes from the small, everyday moments of life. These anecdotes, passed down through generations, capture the essence of the county's humour: bold, energetic, and always ready to find the funny side of any situation.

One well-known story involves a local man who was notorious for his ability to talk his way out of any situation. One day, after being stopped by a police officer for speeding, the man launched into a long-winded explanation about how his car's speedometer was faulty, how the road signs had been confusing, and how he had only been speeding to avoid being late for a very important appointment. The officer listened patiently, then replied with a grin, "You'd talk the hind legs off a donkey, wouldn't you?" The man, realising he wasn't going to get away with it this time, laughed and accepted his ticket, much to the amusement of the officer.

Another popular anecdote tells of a local farmer who, after being asked how his crops were doing, responded with a deadpan expression, "Sure, they'd be grand if the rabbits didn't think they were invited to the dinner table." The dry delivery of the line, combined with the farmer's resigned acceptance of his situation, perfectly captures the kind of humour that thrives in Tyrone—practical, direct, and always ready to find the humour in life's challenges.

Humour and history in Tyrone: Laughter as resilience

County Tyrone, like much of Northern Ireland, has seen its share of political and social upheaval over the years. From the Troubles to economic challenges, the people of Tyrone have faced many difficulties, but through it all, they have maintained their sense of humour. In many ways, humour has been a tool of resilience for the people of Tyrone, helping them to cope with adversity and find strength in laughter.

One of the key features of Tyrone's humour is its ability to deflate tension. In a county where political divisions have often run deep, humour has served as a way to bring people together, allowing them to laugh at themselves and each other in a spirit of camaraderie. Whether it's a joke about the weather, a playful insult, or a story about a local character, humour in Tyrone has always been a way to bridge divides and remind people of their shared humanity.

The people of Tyrone are known for their toughness and their ability to endure difficult times, and their humour reflects this resilience. It's a humour that refuses to back down, that takes on life's challenges with a grin and a quick-witted remark. In Tyrone, laughter isn't just a way to pass the time—it's a way of surviving and thriving in the face of whatever life throws their way.

As we wrap up our exploration of Tyrone's unique sense of humour, it's clear that the county's wit is a reflection of its people—bold, resilient, and deeply connected to the land. From its sharp-tongued banter to its love of practical jokes and wordplay, Tyrone's humour is steeped in the rhythms of rural life and the challenges that come with it. Yet, even in the face of adversity, Tyrone's people have always found ways to laugh, using humour not just as a form of entertainment, but as a tool of survival and a way to bring the community together.

Tyrone's humour, like its landscapes, is full of contrasts—earthy yet sophisticated, cutting yet warm. It thrives on the small moments of everyday life, where a clever quip or a well-timed prank can lift the spirits and strengthen the bonds between friends and neighbours. Whether it's in the bustling pubs of Omagh or the quiet farms that dot the countryside, Tyrone's humour continues to be a vital part of its cultural identity, a reminder that no matter how tough life gets, there's always room for laughter.

With Tyrone's legacy of storytellers, comedians, and everyday jokers, the county's humour lives on, shaping not only its local identity but contributing to the broader tapestry of Northern Irish humour. As we move forward, it's time to step back and see how the humour of each county we've explored—Antrim, Armagh, Derry/Londonderry, Down, Fermanagh, and Tyrone—comes together to form the unique, vibrant, and diverse comedic identity that defines Northern Ireland as a whole.

> I'll have a chip, a saseej supper an' a pastie bap.

Chapter 7: Bringing It all together – Humour in Northern Irish identity

As we bring our journey through the humour of Northern Ireland to a close, one thing becomes abundantly clear: Northern Irish humour is as rich and varied as the landscape itself. From the sharp tongues of Antrim to the playful sarcasm of Derry/Londonderry, from the dry wit of Armagh to the warmth of Down, and from the quirkiness of Fermanagh to the earthy humour of Tyrone, each county has its own distinct flavour of comedy. Yet, despite these differences, there's a shared thread that runs through all of Northern Ireland's humour—a resilience, a cleverness, and an ability to find joy and laughter even in the darkest of times.

The role of humour in Northern Irish life

To truly understand Northern Irish humour, one must first appreciate the role it plays in everyday life. For centuries, humour has been a way for the people of this region to navigate the complexities of their history, culture, and politics. In a place where conflict and division have often been a part of life, humour serves as both a coping mechanism and a bridge, helping people to laugh at their troubles and, in doing so, find common ground.

Northern Irish humour is rarely superficial. It's clever, layered, and often self-deprecating, with a unique ability to poke fun at sensitive issues without crossing the line into malice. This balance is what makes the humour of Northern Ireland so powerful—it disarms tension, diffuses conflict, and brings people together, even in the face of deep-seated differences.

Historical context: Humour as resilience

Throughout Northern Ireland's tumultuous history, humour has been a constant source of resilience. During the darkest days of the Troubles, when fear and uncertainty gripped the region, humour was often the only way for people to make sense of the chaos around them. Jokes, satire, and banter became tools for survival, allowing people to maintain their humanity in the midst of violence and division.

One example of this resilience can be seen in the rise of political satire during the Troubles. Comedians like James Young and Jake O'Kane used their platforms to make light of the absurdities of life in a divided society. Their humour was sharp, insightful, and often risky, but it provided a much-needed outlet for both Protestant and Catholic communities to laugh at themselves and each other in a way that was both cathartic and healing.

Even outside of the political sphere, humour was a way for people to connect with one another, to share in the small joys of everyday life. Whether it was a quick-witted exchange in a pub, a playful jab at a neighbour, or a humorous anecdote passed down through generations, humour became a way to create a sense of normalcy in an otherwise chaotic world.

The Common threads: What unites Northern Irish humour

While each county in Northern Ireland has its own distinct comedic style, there are several common threads that unite them all. One of the most notable is the love of banter. In every corner of Northern Ireland, banter is a form of social interaction that is both playful and competitive. It's not just about making jokes; it's about engaging in a back-and-forth exchange of wit, where the goal is to outsmart your opponent with clever comebacks and quick thinking. This kind of verbal sparring is a hallmark of Northern Irish humour, and it reflects the region's deep respect for cleverness and intelligence.

Another common thread is the use of self-deprecation. Northern Irish people are known for their ability to laugh at themselves, and this humility is a key aspect of their humour. Whether they're making fun of their own political divisions, their weather, or their quirks, the people of Northern Ireland are masters at turning the lens inward and finding humour in their own flaws and challenges. This self-awareness is what allows them to navigate difficult topics with grace and humour, creating a sense of solidarity in the face of adversity.

Finally, there's the use of sarcasm and irony, which can be found in every county we've explored. Whether it's the biting sarcasm of Derry/Londonderry or the dry irony of Armagh, Northern Irish humour often relies on saying the opposite of what is meant, forcing the listener to read between the lines and engage with the underlying message. This type of humour requires a sharp mind and a quick wit, and it's a testament to the intellectual nature of Northern Irish comedy.

The future of Northern Irish humour

As Northern Ireland continues to evolve, so too does its humour. In recent years, there has been a new wave of comedians, writers, and performers who are taking the traditional humour of the region and adapting it to a modern context. Comedians like Diona Doherty, Shane Todd, and Paddy Raff are part of this new generation, blending the wit and banter of their predecessors with fresh perspectives on contemporary life in Northern Ireland.

These new voices are tackling everything from social media to the changing political landscape, all while staying true to the core elements of Northern Irish humour—cleverness, resilience, and the ability to find laughter in the everyday. As Northern Ireland becomes more globally connected, its humour is also reaching new audiences, showcasing the unique wit of the region to the world.

Humour as a unifying force

At its heart, humour in Northern Ireland is about connection. Whether it's through banter, storytelling, or shared laughter, humour has always been a way for people to bridge divides, break down barriers, and find common ground. In a place where political and cultural differences have often created tension, humour serves as a reminder of the things that unite us all—our humanity, our ability to laugh, and our need for connection.

In the end, the humour of Northern Ireland is more than just jokes and laughter—it's a reflection of the people themselves. It's a testament to their strength, their resilience, and their enduring spirit. From the streets of Belfast to the shores of Lough Neagh, from the hills of Fermanagh to the bustling pubs of Derry, humour is woven into the fabric of Northern Irish life, reminding us all that, no matter what challenges we face, there will always be room for laughter.

Conclusion

As we look back on our journey through the humour of Northern Ireland, it's clear that each county contributes something unique to the region's comedic identity. Yet, despite these differences, there's a shared sense of wit, resilience, and cleverness that binds them all together. Northern Irish humour is a powerful force, one that has helped its people navigate their history, celebrate their culture, and, most importantly, connect with one another.

In a world that is often divided, Northern Irish humour offers a reminder of the power of laughter to heal, to unite, and to bring joy. And as long as there are people in Northern Ireland, there will always be humour—a sharp-tongued, quick-witted, and wonderfully resilient humour that continues to bring people together, one joke at a time.

Printed by Amazon Italia Logistica S.r.l.
Torrazza Piemonte (TO), Italy